# *Lightning in a Throttle*

## How Three EVs Set Some of the Earliest Auto Racing Records

## Kristen Hall-Geisler

Copyright © 2016 by Kristen Hall-Geisler

All rights reserved. This book or any portion thereof may not be reproduced or used in any manner whatsoever without the express written permission of the publisher except for the use of brief quotations in a book review.

Printed in the United States of America

ISBN : 978-1-7320603-6-4

Practical Fox LLC

PO Box 83188

Portland OR 97283

www.PracticalFox.com

# Contents

Preface

Overview

1. Andrew Riker Takes an Early Lead

2. Camille Jenatzy Is Never Content

3. Walter Baker Torpedoes Road Racing

4. Conclusion: What Does History Show Us About the Future of Electric Road Racing?

Notes

# Preface

The spark of the idea for *Lightning in a Throttle* came in 2007, when I was reporting on the tenth anniversary of the National Electric Drag Racing Association for the *New York Times*. I'd been updating the newspaper's online automotive calendar for about a year when I pitched this event, which would be held at Portland International Raceway, to my editor, Norman Mayersohn. He assigned the story based on my budding journalistic skills, my track record for meeting deadlines, and probably most importantly, he thought it sounded ridiculous. In 2007, it kind of was.

I had a blast talking to these guys. There weren't any commercially available, daily-driver electric cars on the market then. There were little glorified golf carts like the Zap!, but there were no Chevy Bolts ore Tesla Model S sedans or Kia Soul EVs then. Hybrids like the Prius were still gaining traction with shoppers, and people were skeptical of lithium-ion batteries. We didn't even have smartphones.

But the men (they were almost all men) of NEDRA were building electric cars to leave gassers, as they called internal-combustion-engined vehicles, waiting at the starting line, victims of their own power bands. There is no rev to an EV; there is only immediate torque. When you press the accelerator, all the power is available immediately. You can silently burn down a drag strip in a homemade converted EV faster than most blown Mustangs can imagine. Watching the spectators was as much fun as watching the drags.

As a freelance automotive journalist, I went on to write about EVs both fast and slow for *Popular Science, How Stuff Works, TechCrunch,* and *Mental Floss*. I wrote several pieces on electric vehicles for the *Times*, including a record-setting motorcycle and a startup based in Eugene, Oregon, with celebrity cachet from actor Nathan Fillion of *Castle* and *Firefly*. I'm lucky enough to live in a state that's working to embrace EVs as quickly as possible, so I've been able to drive nearly every available electric car as it becomes available.

But even as electric vehicles improve in capability, efficiency, and range per charge, they still carry a reputation for being poky and no fun, the good-for-you kale of the car world when you really want pizza. Race series like Formula E are bringing speed and sexiness to electric vehicles, but there's a century of preconceptions to overcome.

I knew that electric cars were built in serious numbers in the early days of the automobile, so it stood to reason that these cars ran races—and maybe even won. That's how I found out about the three men whose EV racing stories are detailed here: the proto-hipster, the Belgian boundary breaker, and the mad scientist. Like all the best racing stories, these guys were insanely competitive and unafraid of being originals.

Their stories can help lift the burden EVs carry of being good for you and boring. These three tales of old-timey derring-do prove that EVs are anything but boring—and sometimes not good for you. Just ask the victims of Bad Luck Baker's "Freak Machine." Yeah. No less an authority than the *New York Times* called it the Freak Machine.

## OVERVIEW

In the early years of the automobile, it was not entirely clear that gasoline was going to be the big winner—on the track or in the marketplace. Inventors and manufacturers in these first decades pursued gasoline, diesel, steam, and electric propulsion, each with some degree of success.

Racing in these days pitted propulsion systems against one another. There were classes for each type, and later divisions for weights and body styles within those classes, but they all ran on the same tracks and often at the same time. This is where electric cars had an advantage: all torque, all the time. Mashing the throttle of an electric vehicle (EV), then as now, delivered off-the-line power that gasoline and steam cars couldn't match.

There were some problems, though, like the fact that electric vehicles delivered none of the thrilling roar that gasoline engines did as they raced. The inability of electric race cars to go more than a few laps at top speed meant that when races got longer, EVs were out of the picture. Again, then as now.

In this book, I will detail the contributions of three early racer-inventors to electric vehicle history and conclude by connecting their achievements to electric racing's resurgence more than a hundred years later.

I will first discuss Andrew Riker, a Brooklyn inventor and entrepreneur who successfully raced his own inventions for years and founded the Riker Electric Vehicle Company. But even he would abandon electric vehicles to work on gasoline engines at Locomobile and later become the first president of the Society of Automotive

Engineers, now known as SAE.

Next I'll turn to Camille Jenatzy, a Belgian inventor and devoted racer, who traded world record times with a French count in 1899. Jenatzy won in the end by breaking the 100 km/h barrier in the *Jamais Contente*—twice in the same day, just to prove his point. But he too would abandon electric vehicles and finish his career as a driver for the Mercedes-Benz racing team.

Finally, there's Walter C. Baker, who raced to notoriety in the Baker Torpedo in 1902. It was his electric vehicle at this race that likely did in street-course racing in America. He lost control of the Torpedo and ran into a crowd of bystanders, a few of whom died as a result. Baker didn't give up, though; he continued to refine the Torpedo's design and raced several versions of his electric vehicles over the next few years—on tracks.

In the conclusion, I'll discuss how these early races and racers are echoed today, particularly in Formula E racing, but also in purpose-built record setters.

# 1. Andrew Riker Takes an Early Lead

## THE EARLIEST RACES

Car people are fond of saying that the first race was run when the second car was built. That's nearly true. While dozens of engineers and hobbyists all over the world had their hands in the automobile invention pie at the end of the nineteenth century, credit for the first real automobile is generally given to Karl Benz for his gasoline-powered three-wheeler in 1885. But the first electric vehicle actually came a bit earlier, when Gustave Trouvé powered up an electric tricycle in France in 1881. The first-ever staged automobile race was run from Paris to Rouen, a distance of 128 km, in 1894. But these clacking, gasoline-powered machines were so smelly, noisy, and new that no one took much of a shine to this mechanical sideshow.

As the historian and automotive engineer Ernest Henry Wakefield pointed out, "In an incredibly short period, public sentiment for the automobile changed from indifference to enthusiasm. What ignited the fuse was the second automobile race."[1] For this second competition, in 1895, entrants raced from Paris to Bordeaux and back again—that race had an electric automobile driven by Charles Jeantaud at the starting line. It only ran the course one way rather than making the round trip that the gasoline- and steam-powered cars took. Jeantaud had to set up charging stations in advance, spaced at forty-mile intervals, in order to achieve his average speed of 14.4 mph along the 705-mile route.[2]

This second automobile race pricked up ears around the globe. In America, it spurred the creation of *Horseless Age,* the first periodical to be dedicated to motorcars—not that anyone could agree on proper terminology in the first year of publication. Should the fuel used in combustion engines be "gasoline" or "gasolene"?[3] Should the person operating the motor carriage be called a "driver," like the guy who held the horses' reins and steered the car, or a "chauffeur," after the French word for the guy who stoked steam engines?[4]

## THE FIRST AMERICAN RACE

Using the French as their model, the *Chicago Times-Herald* staged the first American road race from Chicago to Evanston and back in 1895. In November. In Illinois. This was a terrible idea.

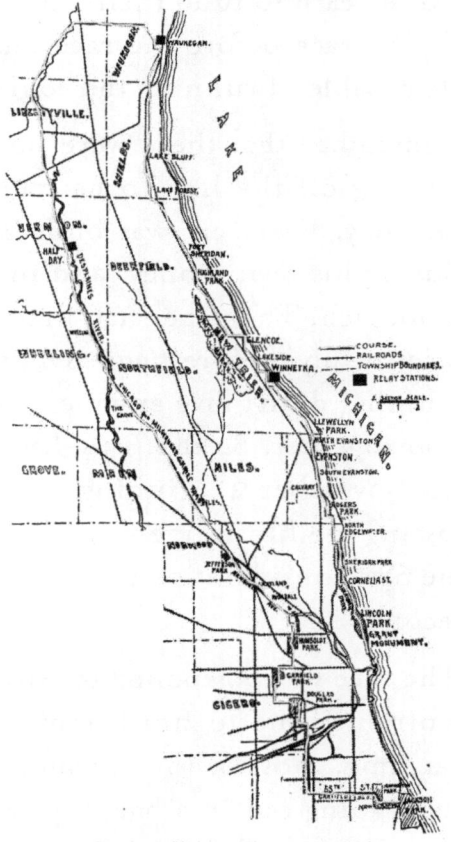

ROUTE OF ROAD RACE. (*Chicago Times-Herald.*)

*The Chicago race course, take one.*

The first issue of *Horseless Age* printed a map of the course and the rules of the race. There was a lengthy list of entries for the November 2 race and notification of $5,000 total in prize money,[5] which lit a fire under the inventors who needed the cash to fund their automotive ambitions. The race before the race was to finish a vehicle capable of running the course.

Remember that there were no ready-made cars rolling off the line to be merely prepped for race day. Every car was built by a guy in a shop using his own money, and inventors were often not rich. The paper had first tried to hold the race in July, before *Horseless Age* was publishing, but that didn't give anyone enough time to get a car together. So the *Times-Herald* moved the date to November 2. Winning was not a matter of crossing the finish line first; "general utility" was the first consideration to be judged. "Speed" was second.

The race was postponed to November 28 to give entrants time to finish their vehicles, but by that time, most of the entrants had thought better of going out in a barely proven, roofless motor carriage in the winter. Only eight entries were listed in the next issue of *Horseless Age,* which also printed another map of the route, noting that the track would not be cleared of pedestrians or other traffic. Horses, carts, streetcars—racers would have to contend with all of them. At least the streetcar tracks were helpfully noted on the map. "Nothing but a severe snowstorm can render the route unfit for the test," the unsuperstitious magazine said.

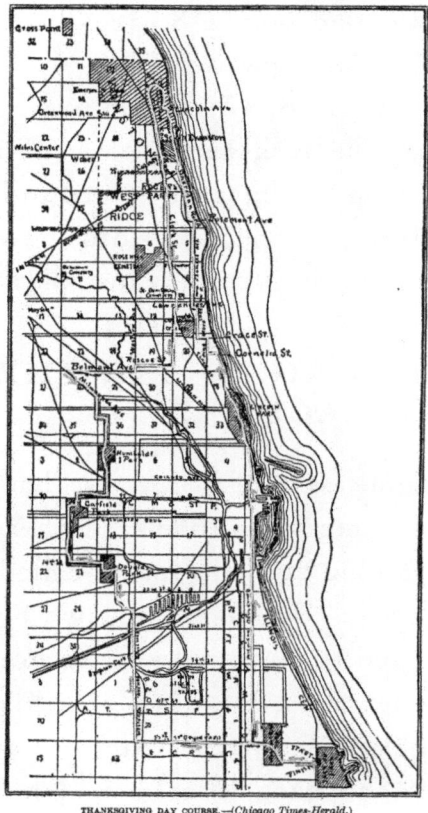

*The Chicago race course, take two.*

Fate being tempted, she had no choice but to answer. Six inches of snow and slush covered the ground, and only six racers made it to the starting line. So while an electric vehicle driven by a Harold Sturges did enter the race, it only managed to push through thirteen miles of snowy road before Sturges likely ran out of profanities and gave up. The *New York Times* said, "This race, if not a Waterloo, was a very serious setback." The track wasn't cleared of traffic, either, so racers had to maneuver around horses and their carriages. Spectators did show up to watch the race, but they threw snowballs at the racers.

## ANDREW RIKER AND THE FIRST TRACK RACE

In the same issue of *Horseless Age* that reported on this snowy mess of a road race, there is a photograph of a kid on contraption called an "electric motor cycle."[6] He has taken two bicycle frames and welded them together with horizontal bars as wide as he is. He has a seat high above the wheels, a box full of batteries, and a motor between the back wheels, and he's holding a lever for controlling the speed of the thing in his right hand. Though he's obviously young and clean-shaven in this photo, inventor Andrew L. Riker has already created the Riker Electric Motor Company, and this is merely his first prototype.

ELECTRIC MOTOR CYCLE.   ANDREW L. RIKER, BROOKLYN, N. Y.

*Andrew L. Riker, proto-hipster.*

Things really got cranking for automobiles when the Americans put their stamp on racing by staging events on tracks. Europe had fairly decent roads to travel along, and so Continental racers preferred the point-to-point rally style of competition. Americans had terrible roads, and driving a car along them for any distance was a miserable experience at any speed. But we had pretty nice racetracks for horses.

The first American automobile track race was announced for September 7, 1896, on the one-mile Narragansett horse track at the fairgrounds in Cranston, Rhode Island, again with $5,000 in prizes to be awarded.[7] There would be five heats, one each weekday of the fair being held that week. Each heat would be five laps, for a total of five miles each day. As in horse racing, contestants had to run in all the heats in order to win the full purse. "As the course is ideal for electric vehicles," said an editor of *Horseless Age*, "we may expect to see some lively brushes between them and the gasoline wagons."[8]

This expectation drew a reported 60,000 spectators in the grandstands over the five days of the fair[9]—mostly fair-goers who thought it might be fun to watch these newfangled machines run at breakneck speeds around the dirt track as a break from inspecting the prizewinning pigs and pies.

Andrew Riker had by this time earned a reputation as the builder of "the fastest electric vehicles for track racing," according to Wakefield.[10] Being a proto-hipster who'd dropped out of Columbia University to build an electric vehicle factory in Brooklyn, Riker had also grown a mustache by this time. By 1899, his company would have $7 million in capital.[11] He would change its name to Riker Electric Vehicle Company and begin building entire cars, not just electric motors, in Elizabethtown, New Jersey.

Riker's vehicle in the 1896 Narragansett race weighed 1,500 pounds, about the weight of one of the mature Holsteins at the fair. Over half the car's weight was due to the 32 chloride battery cells, which totaled about 800 pounds all by themselves. The car had two 3-hp electric motors, each powering a rear wheel, and four speeds—each way. When it wasn't under the heavy load of racing, the setup had a range of 4 hours at 10 mph.[12]

Twelve cars of various propulsion systems registered for the race, but five withdrew because the minimum required speed was 24 km/h[13]—all of 15 mph—and they couldn't cut it. (No wonder skeptics and naysayers in the crowd yelled, "Get a horse!" A horse at full gallop can easily reach twice that speed.) On race day, under darkening clouds, seven cars lined up at the starting line: five gasoline-powered vehicles and two electric-powered. They were all open buggies with tall, skinny, spoked wheels.

*The Narragansett starting line.*

The first two days' heats went well. Riker took the pole, with another electric car taking the second position at the starting line. Riker ran the first heat on Monday in 15:01, a respectable but not winning time. The second day, he ran the five miles in 13:06 and won the heat.[14] All the teams had learned lessons the first day, though, and all dropped their times significantly.

But it turned out that weather was again not going to be a racer's friend, even in August. A storm rolled in, and the heats for Wednesday and Thursday were cancelled. Track racing was even newer than road racing, so no provisions were made for a parc expose or concours-type event so people could examine these newfangled autos when they weren't on the track or in the garage. The gasoline cars and electric cars were housed more than a mile apart from each other in barns, since the fair's management didn't think to set up any charging equipment for batteries near the track. The electric racers had to make do with what electric outlets they could find in an unused barn far from the interested crowds.

The heats resumed on Friday, with Riker racing five miles in 11:28[15]—coming over the finish line one frustrating second behind the Electric Carriage & Wagon Company's car. When the data were analyzed, Riker's car had set the record for fastest mile in 2:13 and his top speed was nearly 27 mph, earning the Riker Electric Motor Company first prize.[16]

"The blood of the contestants was now up," reported *Horseless Age*, "and all were bent on smashing records on Saturday."[17] But there were horse races scheduled for Saturday, and fair management could not or would not move them. The horse racers were already a bit miffed that the automobile racing purses were larger than theirs. But because the car racers had only raced three out of five heats, they were each given 3/5 of the purses, as would be awarded in horse races.[18] But horse racers don't need money to invent and build their horses.

Reporting on the last day of the races, *Scientific American* said,

> The announcement of the success of the electric carriages created some surprise, as it has been thought lately that motors using some form of petroleum were best adapted for horseless carriage use, and the electric motor has been somewhat discounted.[19]

The crowd perceived the noisy, belching, gasoline-powered cars as faster than the quiet electric cars—even though the two electric cars that ran scorched the Narragansett track. *Scientific American* also noted that the electric Riker vehicle in particular was easier to control, quieter, and less smelly than the gasoline-powered cars, which would "commend it to those who are anxious to purchase horseless carriages."[20] But the reporter wasn't sure if the electric vehicle would be of any use over long runs. Range anxiety, it turns out, has been with us for more than a century.

# AMERICA'S FIRST ENDURANCE RACE

Riker reduced some potential buyers' range anxiety a few years later at America's first endurance race, held on April 14, 1900. There were fifteen entries, but in these early days of fickle power trains, only nine made it to the starting line on Long Island in New York. The cars were to run twenty-five miles out and back again along Merrick Road between Springfield and Babylon.[21]

At this race, Riker's electric car carried 60 cell batteries and weighed about 2,500 pounds, making it the heaviest in the race. *Horseless Age* reported that he used 125 volts as he cruised to an easy victory.[22] According to the *New York Times* coverage of the race, "As Mr. Riker came dashing over the finish line, his body bent forward as though holding the reins over some spirited steed, a mighty cheer went up from the throng of enthusiasts."[23] He clocked in at 2:03:30, fifteen minutes ahead of the second-place racer in his gasoline automobile. That poor sap had to stop to add water to his overheating engine twice.[24]

As in racing today, the Merrick Road race was followed by an inspection to make sure no one cheated (though racing days were so early, and cars so hand-built and non-uniform, how could the inspectors tell?). Officials found that the paint around the batteries on Riker's car was scorched, but otherwise the car was in fine shape. Riker even boasted that he could make it back to New York City, which the *Times* reporter seemed skeptical of, but Riker and his wife, Edith, did motor off to Jamaica after the race, which is near Manhattan.[25]

Fifty miles was a milestone, even if two hours seems like a long time to traverse that distance. Most of the electric cars of the time could only drive twenty or thirty miles on a charge.[26] For perspective, the best-selling EV on the road in 2014 was the Nissan Leaf, which the EPA said would officially travel eighty-four miles on a charge.[27]

## THE CONEY ISLAND SPEED TEST

In November of 1901, Riker was back on the track with another electric car called the Torpedo Racer. All the entries in this Coney Island race, which included eight gasoline-powered cars and six steamers, were stripped to just their frames and wheels to decrease weight. In this minimalist trim, Riker's Torpedo Racer, the only electric-powered car to run that day, made 13–15 hp from 900 pounds of lead-zinc batteries.[28]

The Coney Island Automobile Club held its speed test on an old, unused strip of Ocean Parkway, yet 50,000 spectators were reported in the *New York Times* to have lined the route—and sometimes crossed it, not realizing fully the danger they were putting themselves in.[29]

Racers got a quarter-mile flying start before the real starting line marked the beginning of the one-mile straight course. Well, it was straight but still not flat or even. The gasoline cars flew along the course at nearly 70 mph, and when they hit a slight depression or rise, there were reports that all four wheels left the road.[30]

Competitors were racing only the clock rather than other cars, so starts were staggered. Riker had his car towed to the beginning of the quarter-mile so as not to waste one single electron. He didn't win outright this time; that honor went to a gasoline-powered car that flew down the track in under a minute. But Riker did set a world record for electric vehicles by averaging 57.1 mph during his 63-second run. (The steam-powered "winner" in its division trundled in at 1:39.)[31] "That a gasoline carriage would make the best record was inevitable," said *Scientific American,* "but no one foresaw that an electric car would also lower the previous world's record of 1 minute 6 2-5 seconds."[32]

This was Riker's final race, and its results point toward the near-future for both automobiles and racing. The *Times* and *Horseless Age* noted that the Long Island Automobile Club ran the race poorly. The pneumatic tube that was to serve as the starter for timing didn't work, delaying the start of the race by two hours while it was fixed.[33] Add to that delay the ten or fifteen minutes between each car, by the last few racers they were using their headlamps in the darkening autumn evening. As the *Times* reporter put it, "It was the more surprising when the utter lack of management on the part of the Long Island automobilists was discovered. In plain words, it displayed no management."

This lack of organization or control led to near misses at the end of the race course with motorists who weren't racing and, as stated above, spectators wandering about. This lack of crowd control cast a shadow over another race held two years later on Staten Island, where Walter Baker and his Torpedo literally ran into this very problem.

Riker was an automotive specialist, but he was an innovator in all three of the propulsion systems vying for hearts and minds—and wallets. He began with electricity, dabbled in steam, and in 1902 he closed the doors of his own company and joined Locomobile to develop their internal combustion engines. Three years later, he was one of the cofounders of the Society of Automotive Engineers (SAE), and he served as the society's first president.

## 2. Camille Jenatzy Is Never Content

While Andrew Riker was developing his electric vehicles and proving them on America's racetracks, the Belgian son of a rubber goods manufacturer was blowing speed records to smithereens in France. Camille Jenatzy was an engineer from Brussels with a handful of automotive patents to his name and an electric car company of his own, Compagnie Generale des Transports Automobiles Jenatzy.[34] Like Riker and nearly every man in the automotive industry in the late 1800s, Jenatzy had the imagination to invent and the knack to start a company. But what he really had was a competitive spirit.

Jenatzy's company made taxis used in Paris, but Jenatzy made race cars for himself. The race car for which he became world famous was the *Jamais Contente,* "Never Satisfied." Rumor had it that he named it after his mother-in-law,[35] but given how hard he raced that car, and how many records he set with it over a matter of weeks, it just as likely applies to Jenatzy himself.

## TRADING RECORDS

In December 1898, Paul Meyan, editor of *La France Automobile,* announced that the magazine would stage a race for the fastest kilometer.[36] The two-kilometer course would be in Archeres, on the bank of the Seine. An official would give the start signal, and there would be timers at the first and second kilometer marks.

Most of the contestants who took on the two kilometers that December 18 topped out at 25–30 km/h, or 15–18 mph. So when Le Compte Gaston Chasseloup-Laubat showed up with his fancy name and his electric Jeantaud race car and blew everyone away at 64.154 km/h,[37] he was the hero of the hour. He ran the flying kilometer in 57 seconds, which translates to 39.24 mph, more than twice what any other competitor could do. It was more than three times the first speed limit in America, which wouldn't be set until 1901. It was fast. It was also the first officially recognized land speed record, as recognized by Guinness World Records.[38]

And that would have been good enough. The people were amazed, Chasseloup-Laubat probably drank free champagne for a week, and Meyan at *La France Automobile* was happy with the outcome. But the next day, he got a letter from Camille Jenatzy saying he was sorry he hadn't been able to take part in the race. Would M. Chasseloup-Laubat allow him to challenge the record?

Meyan knew who Jenatzy was; he was the engineer with a few patents to his name and the company that built taxis. Jenatzy had entered his first race in November 1898, a hill climb, and won it with a blistering average speed of 17 mph.[39] A head-to-head speed test between Chasseloup-Laubat and Jenatzy would be huge.

On January 17, 1899, Jenatzy and Chasseloup met at the race site. Chasseloup drove an off-the-shelf Jeantaud electric car; Jenatzy brought a car built by his own company.

Since he was the challenger, Jenatzy raced first on that January day. He hit 66 km/h, or just over 41 mph,[40] setting a new world record for any car, not just electric cars.

Hopefully Jenatzy's victory choreography was short, because his record only stood for a few minutes. That fancy villain Le Compte Chausseloup-Laubat turned in a kilometer at 70 km/h, or 43.69 mph, despite his motor blowing 200 yards from the finish line.[41] The day was over. Chausseloup had won.

But not for long! Ten days later, the two were back at Archeres for another go. Jenatzy, still the challenger, flew the two kilometers first and set a new world record: 49.92 mph.[42] Chausseloup's Jeantaud suffered another mechanical failure and did not post a time that day. Jenatzy's record stood.

But not for long! Chausseloup was not only Jenatzy's racing rival, he was his taxi manufacturing rival. They weren't merely racing for prize money; they were racing for fleet contracts far more lucrative than a few hundred francs. They were racing for PR.

On March 4, Chausseloup brought a Jeantaud he had clad in some aerodynamic sheeting. It worked—he turned in a time a hair over 92 km/h, or 57.6 mph. That was very near 100 km/h, which conventional wisdom said the human body could not withstand.[43] Who better to test that limit than two of the fastest race car drivers on the planet? Anyone involved in automobiles at this time was of a scientific bent anyway, at least a little bit, so Jenatzy and Chausseloup may have had a soupçon of curiosity mixed in with their bravado. What would happen when we hit 100 km/h?

## LA JAMAIS CONTENT

On March 31, 1899, Jenatzy debuted *la Jamais Contente,* a bullet-shaped torpedo of a vehicle, in Archeres.

The distinctive body was built by Rheims & Auscher.[44] Its wooden undercarriage (a common material for the day) was covered in partinium (an uncommon material for any day), an alloy of aluminum, magnesium, and tungsten.[45] It made for a very light body, only about 450 pounds[46] "so that it plunges through the air like a dart."[47] Though the bullet shape was far more aerodynamic than any other car on the road or track, it wasn't perfect. There was no cockpit. The driver could only fit his legs inside the sleek shape; the rest of him was perched above the shell, adding drag and inviting disaster. Jenatzy crouched low over the fuselage as he piloted the car on the racecourse, rendering the shape of the car useless in aerodynamic terms. It was powered by 100 2-volt Fulmen cells that weighed over 1,400 pounds. Those turned two 25-kW motors mounted on the rear driving-axle that together made 50 hp.[48]

The whole thing was painted blue-gray with flashy red wheels. Its audacious name was emblazoned on its side. This was the world's first purpose-built race car. It could do no other thing besides go very fast over a kilometer. Maybe two. It could do no other thing but be the fastest car in the world.

THE "NEVER CONTENT" OF M. JENATZY.
*Jenatzy in the Jamais Contente*

So on April 29, 1899, Jenatzy brought *la Jamais Contente* to the starting line again. This time, he raced to an official 105.879 km/h—65.79 mph.[49] The fastest vehicle in the world was a bullet-shaped electric car.

And then, for good measure, Jenatzy and *la Jamais Contente* repeated the feat the next day.

*Horseless Age* took note of Jenatzy's accomplishment in its coverage of the race on Long Island that summer: "Riker's speed was less than Jenotzy's [sic] in his record race with the Jamais Contente."[50]

The record did not stand for long, though. Late in the summer of 1901, *Horseless Age* again reported from the racing scene:

> The kilometre, flying start, was made [by S. F. Edge] in 32 2/5 seconds, lowering the record of Jenatzy's Jamais Contente of 34 1/5 seconds and a 5 mile distance was run in 4 minutes 44 3/5 seconds. These speeds are equal to 69 miles and 62.5 miles per hour respectively. The kilometre record has thus passed from an electric to a gasoline machine.

Jenazty had a passion for racing but not, apparently, electric cars. He raced with Mors, a manufacturer of gasoline-powered vehicles. He decided he could build a better racer himself and created a gasoline-electric system for a Bolide, which he drove in the Gordon Bennet Cup race of 1900. Eventually, he found himself driving with the Mercedes-Benz racing team. After a few false starts, he took the Gordon Bennet Cup in 1903—with a 12-minute margin of victory.[51] He continued to race on and off for years, eventually retiring to return to running the family business in Brussels.

# 3. Walter Baker Torpedoes Road Racing

One fine spring day in 1902 Walter C. Baker, builder of electric cars, racer of electric cars, and notorious crasher of his experimental electric cars, brought his latest contender to Staten Island for an attempt at the record of the day, the flying mile. The tall, lanky, daring driver known to some as "Bad Luck Baker"[52] wore his usual tinted goggles in preparation for the race, emphasizing his oddness in a field of odd inventors and engineers.

The car he brought was the latest evolution of his purpose-built racing vehicles. The Baker Motor Vehicle Company, based in Cleveland, built normal, safe electric vehicles for the likes of Thomas Edison, whose first car was indeed a Baker,[53] but those cars were nothing like the race cars. Baker liked to push the envelope; he put the try in trial run. Not every try was a success; in one beach race, all the wheels came off his car.[54]

But sometimes Baker won, and spectacularly. A couple of years previous to this Staten Island race, Baker had entered a race that included a Riker electric that was driven by a man named Ed Adams.[55] Baker's electric vehicle won over Riker's in the obstacle course; later that week Riker's car bested him in the brake contest where vehicles had to prove they could stop in a timely fashion. Really, everything about automobiles was new and worth contesting. At the end of the week, the gasoline, electric, and steam-powered winners of the obstacle course met head to head for a final run through the course. Baker won that too.

## TORPEDO DESIGN

In Staten Island, all bets were on Baker. He brought the specialized racing vehicle known as the Baker Torpedo, a bullet on wheels that weighed a ton and a half. The "demon machine," as spectators were calling it, had cost Baker about $10,000 to build in 1902,[56] which would amount to about $250,000 today.

While the shape of the Torpedo was reminiscent of Camille Jenatzy's *Jamais Contente,* its more pear-shaped design was based on a drop of oil. According to a *Popular Science* profile published in 1916, Baker had noticed one day that a drop of oil was not perfectly round. He surmised that laying a drop on its side and cutting it in half would allow his vehicle to slip through the air with less resistance. [57]

*The Baker Torpedo in better days, courtesy of Scientific American.*

But it wasn't just drops of oil that inspired Baker's design. Steam-power pioneer Leon Serpollet in France built a race car he called the *Oeuf de Pâques,* or Easter Egg.[58] This design plopped a torpedo-shaped body onto the flat platform of the chassis for improved, but not perfect, aerodynamics. The driver and mechanic still sat upright in the cockpit, further negating any aerodynamic gains of the rounded hood. Still, Serpollet did break the 100 km/h barrier in April 1902, the first steam car to do so.[59]

Unlike either of those French racers, Baker and his codriver fit entirely inside the vehicle.

He designed a little "conning tower" with isinglass panels so that he could see where he was going without sacrificing aerodynamics by crouching on top of the smooth exterior. He had webbed seats like little hammocks fitted with canvas straps that acted as a primitive safety harness. Baker as driver sat with his legs in the nose of the car, with a teensy 7-inch steering wheel to hold onto; his codriver Denzer (his first and middle initials were variously given as E. E., C. E., and C. A.), who was in charge of the brakes and batteries, squeezed in behind him.

The Torpedo had one 14-hp motor mounted behind the driver and codriver, with forty lead-zinc batteries arranged on the floor of the chassis. The tops of the 36-inch wheels stood above the low-slung body of the car, and their spokes were covered.[60]

## A RACE GONE WRONG

The race, which was sponsored by the Automobile Club of America, had been given formal permission by the local authorities to run on public streets, specifically South Shore Boulevard, which was paved. There were tracks that crossed the street, which the ACA requested be taken up for the speed contest; they were instead covered over with dirt. Reports said that 20,000 spectators lined the boulevard in hopes of seeing a record being set.[61]

The gasoline and steam racers went before the electric class. Twenty-four "whizzing monsters," as the *New York Times* reporter called them,[62] flew along the one-mile course, ending near Grant City. With each successive contestant racing over the tracks, the dirt was displaced. The cars were slamming into those metal bars with their spindly tires at speed, causing them to skip into the air. One spectator told the *Times* that the cars were "taking the hurdles."[63]

When it was Baker's turn, he and Denzer climbed into their cockpit and settled themselves back to back. As with other speed contests, there was a run-up to the official start and then a runoff to allow the racers to slow down. The Baker Torpedo got up a great head of speed right from the start, covering the first six-tenths of a mile in 36 seconds.[64]

By some reports, the Torpedo was already swerving down the road as it approached the trolley track at Lincoln Avenue. There was a gentle chicane in the course, and Baker lost control on the curve. Then he hit that trolley track, the one that had sent racers with full control into the air.

To make matters worse, Denzer hit the brakes at the same time—hard.

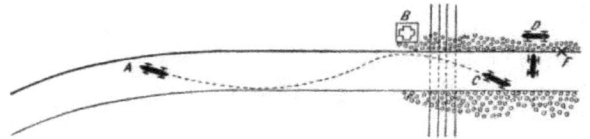

*Caption: Scientific American's diagram of the Torpedo's trajectory.*

The car went airborne, landed, and spun in circles through crowds of spectators. Not that there should have been spectators there at all. The roped-off viewing area was on the right side of the road, but a better view could be had by crossing South Shore Boulevard and standing near some shrubbery. People had been ducking under the rope and crossing the road all day. About sixty people were on the left side of the road when the Torpedo came at them.

"VICTIMS TOSSED IN THE AIR," read the *Times*'s headline.[65] One person, a tax assessor, was killed on the spot, two were mortally wounded,[66] six were seriously injured, and "a score more or less harmed." There were broken legs, bruises, abrasions, and one man was even pinned under the car when it came to rest.

He survived.

Baker and Denzer had those primitive canvas harnesses, so they were mostly okay inside the Torpedo. When they clambered out, they found mild sulfuric acid burns from the batteries were their worst injuries.

The race was immediately stopped. Luckily, the wreck occurred quite near the participants' first aid tent, so many of the injured spectators could be tended to immediately on-site. A wagon loaded with an oblivious ragtime band came trundling down the road soon after, not having gotten the message that the entertainment for the day was done. The *Times* reported that police threatened to club the musicians if they didn't can it.[67]

*The Torpedo on its worst day.*

In the immediate aftermath, Baker didn't appear to know what had happened, exactly. He thought he'd cut the car's power when he lost control, before they hit the tracks. He wondered if a wheel had come off. But it was apparent that all four wheels were on the car where it lay in the grass. In the confusion, Baker and Denzer wandered off and returned to their hotel.

That's where the police found them. They were arrested and charged with homicide, with bail set at $5,000 each,[68] which they posted with a wad of cash bills from Baker's pocket. The men pointed out that they had minor injuries and burns that needed attending, so they were sent to the hospital for treatment under police guard.

In the meantime, the second man died of his injuries from, as the *Times* repeatedly called it, the "Freak Machine." Those who had run for their lives the day before went to the local fire station where the Torpedo had been towed to see the Freak Machine at rest. By all reports, it wasn't in bad shape.[69]

Neither were Baker and Denzer. When they were called before the magistrate on being released from the hospital, Baker had a limp and Denzer had a cut on his head. Denzer told a reporter that he didn't think he'd gotten the wound in the crash but rather from concerned citizens trying to break into the vehicle and help the men out.[70]

Baker told the *Times*, "The first impression I had that all was not right was that I noticed that the crowd was swaying before my eyes from side to side. ... I yelled to Mr. Denzer to hold fast, and then the crash came."[71]

District Attorney Edward Rawson was in the crowd when the Torpedo torpedoed into it. He offered this incredible description:

> Certainly I have never seen anything like it in my life. To see some of the other autos coming along was a sight, but that freak of a thing—well, it only lacked a devil sitting upon it with his forked tail sticking up. ... I saw one man go up into the air and turn a somersault for all the world like an acrobat. He landed on his feet, strange to say, and was not injured.
>
> ... Although the Board of Alderman [of Staten Island] gave permission for the race [to the ACA], I doubt that they had any idea that such a freak as that of Baker's was to be introduced in the race. It would be interesting to learn,

too, why the Automobile Club took the precaution of erecting a Red Cross tent.[72]

What Rawson didn't ask was why he and the others who had been hurt had lifted the flimsy rope barrier and crossed the race route. It didn't take long before the official investigation realized that spectators, including the worked-up district attorney, had crossed the barrier and had been standing in a danger zone. Baker and Denzer were released. Not long after, a third man died of his injuries from the accident.

## THE END OF ROAD RACES

The record for the American mile at the time was 55 seconds. The fastest motorcycle to take on the mile did it in 1:10. The fastest steamer in the world did a mile in 1:12. Baker had bested all of them. But those records would all continue to stand. Because the Torpedo never crossed the finish line (and presumably because it plowed into a crowd of spectators and killed three men), the Staten Island record never counted.

"The Automobile Club of America has decided to hold no more road speed tests of automobiles in the future," reported *Scientific American*.[73] Even a friend of Baker's who was asked for a quote by a *Times* reporter when leaving the station after the racers' arrest, said, "Well, this ends automobile racing on Staten Island."[74]

Not only did it end racing in Staten Island, it also put the final nail in coffin of American road racing. Where Europe developed rally racing and street courses, the United States took racing from the streets to proper tracks. Even drag racing was moved from stoplights to drag strips with the formation of the National Hot Rod Association.

But racing didn't end for Walter C. Baker. He was back at it in Detroit on October 24 and 25, 1902, though not with the Torpedo.[75] He did race the Torpedo twice the next year, inspiring this bit of ominous prose from *Horseless Age:* "A big white torpedolike monster glided silently down the track and retired after making two turns."[76] In 1903, he had entered the lighter Torpedo Kid with a D. Chisholm as driver in a race when it flew off the track and through a fence at about 30 mph. The car hit four people, one of whom swooned and fainted. Luckily, none of the injuries this time were fatal, or even serious.[77] This proved to be the final race for Bad Luck Baker.

# Conclusion: What Does History Show Us about the Future of Electric Racing?

With the resure of electric vehicles has come electric vehicle racing. The echoes of the turn of the last century are evident, even to the announcement of Formula E adding a race in Brooklyn for the 2016–17 season, stomping grounds for both Andrew Riker and Walter Baker.

Not that Formula E seems to be interested in the historic significance of its choice. The reason Brooklyn was chosen, along with every other city around the globe where it holds races, is that a street course in an urban center has been approved. The head of the series, Alejandro Agag, wants to put electric racing where the people are,[78] and the people are moving to the cities. By 2050, the World Health Organization predicts that two-thirds of the world's population will live in urban areas, adding, "Between now and then, the population of cities will nearly double."[79]

The WHO is not interested in racing; it's interested in the health effects of this density. But Agag and the FIA see it as bringing racing to where the people are. This is an easier task in Europe, South America, and Asia, where street courses are not unusual. It's more of a challenge in the United States. For the first two seasons, Long Beach, California, hosted the series on a modified version of its decades-old street course as a warm-up to the Indy grand prix race. But Long Beach has been cut from the schedule for the third season, as Miami was cut after one race in the first season.

Urban racing is possible in the twenty-first century because the cars are electric. They have zero emissions, so there are fewer complaints about pollution from the people who live in the city. The cars are also quieter, which generates fewer complaints from neighbors and more complaints from race fans—just as it did at the first track race in 1896. I interviewed fans in the paddock at the first Long Beach Formula E race in 2015, and they almost all mentioned the lack of noise as something they didn't like or would have to adjust to.[80] Track officials are already adjusting—they blow whistles on the pit lane to alert everyone to the presence of a quiet electric race car approaching.

It is possible that Formula E and its electric race cars—including the driverless Roborace series set to debut in 2017—will bring street course racing back to the United States. It's also possible, in the long term, that all gasoline-powered racing will be relegated to the tracks outside cities and be treated as vintage racing rather than the cutting edge.

There are also inheritors of Jenatzy's relentless pursuit of records. The Buckeye Bullet, a joint project of electric vehicle developer Venturi and Ohio State University, just broke its own record for fastest electric vehicle on September 22, 2016. The long, pointed vehicle reached 341.4 mph on the Bonneville Salt Flats, beating the previous record of 307.7 set in 2010.

That's more than a 100 mph faster than the fastest production car,[81] but it's far short of the current land speed record. A turbo jet-powered vehicle known as ThrustSSC holds that title at 763.035 mph. That's Mach 1.016.[82]

The glass-half-empty reader will conclude that electric vehicles are doomed to being underpowered putterers about town, but the glass-half-full reader will see this as proof that there is vast room for improvement. Engineering batteries and electric drivetrains to have the necessary power and the ability to withstand the immense amounts of torque required in these record-setting runs, as well as the street courses of Formula E races, will only benefit the consumer electric car market. The old NASCAR slogan, "Race on Sunday, drive on Monday," may belong to electric cars in the future.

# Notes

1  Ernest Henry Wakefield, PhD., *History of the Electric Automobile: Battery-Only Powered Cars*. (Warrendale, PA: Society of Automotive Engineers, 1994) 1.

2  Ibid.

3  "The Providence Race." *The Horseless Age* 1, no. 10 (August 1896): 1.

4  Ray Stannard Baker, *The Boys' Book of Modern Inventions* (McClure, Phillips & Co.: 1906), 169.

5  Ibid.

6  "The Riker Electric Trap." *The Horseless Age* 1, no. 10 (August 1896): 18–20.

7  "The Rhode Island State Fair Offers Substantial Prizes." *The Horseless Age* 1, no. 6 (1894 and 1895): 15–16.

8  "The Providence Race." *The Horseless Age* 1, no. 10 (August 1896): 1.

9  "This Day in History, September 7: Electric car wins the first auto race in the United States." History, accessed April 2015. http://www.history.com/this-day-in-history/electric-car-wins-the-first-auto-race-in-the-united-states.

10  Wakefield, *History of the Electric Automobile*, 61.

11  Ibid.

12  "The Riker Electric Trap." *The Horseless Age* 1, no. 10 (August 1896): 18–20.

13  "Official Rules of the Rhode Island Race and Exhibition." *The Horseless Age* 1, no. 9 (July 1896): 16.

14  "The Race Track." *The Horseless Age* 1, no. 11 (September 1896): 1–2, 6–7.

15  Ibid.

16  "The Providence Horseless Carriage Race."

Scientific American, September 26, 1896, 253.

17   "The Race Track." The Horseless Age 1, no. 11 (September 1896): 1–2, 6–7.

18   Ibid.

19   Scientific American, "The Providence Race."

20   Ibid.

21   "The Automobile Club's First Race." The Horseless Age 6, no. 3 (April 18, 1900): 10.

22   Ibid.

23   "First Automobile Fifty-Mile Race Ever Run in America," New York Times, April 15, 1900.

24   Ibid.

25   Ibid.

26   Ibid.

27   Sebastian Blanco, "Number of Electric Vehicles Doubling Every Year." Autoblog, April 1, 2014. http://www.autoblog.com/2014/04/01/number-of-electric-vehicles-doubling-every-year/.

28   Wakefield, History of the Electric Automobile, 242.

29   "New Automobile Records," New York Times, November 17, 1901.

30   "New Automobile Speed Records," Scientific American, November 30, 1901, 347.

31   Wakefield, History of the Electric Automobile, 242.

32   "New Automobile Speed Records," Scientific American, November 30, 1901, 347.

33   "The Long Island Automobile Club's Races." The Horseless Age 8, no. 43 (November 20, 1901): 735–739.

34   "La Jamais Contente Caracteristiques techniques." Lions District 103 and Energie Ouest Su-

isse, Accessed May 3, 2015. http://www.e-mobile.ch/pdf/2005/Fact-Sheet_LaJamaisContente_FW.pdf.

35    Don Sherman, "Original speed demon: The first car to hit 100km/h." Drive, January 28, 2011. http://www.drive.com.au/motor-news/original-speed-demon-the-first-car-to-hit-100kmh-20110127-1a61m.html.

36    Les Amis de la Jamais Contente, "Les records de vitesse," accessed May 3, 2015. http://la-jamais-contente.e-monsite.com/pages/les-records-de-vitesse.html.

37    Ibid.

38    "First recognized land-speed record." Guinness World Records, accessed January 9, 2016. http://www.guinnessworldrecords.com/world-records/first-recognized-land-speed-record.

39    Vanderbilt Cup Races. "Camille Jenatzy." Driver Bio, accessed May 3, 2015. http://www.vanderbiltcupraces.com/drivers/bio/camile_jenatzy.

40    Ibid.

41    Ibid.

42    Martyn Goddard, "First to Sixty: La Jamais Contente." Automobile, January 3, 2011. http://www.automobilemag.com/features/news/1102_la_jamais_contente/.

43    Ibid.

44    Vanderbilt Cup Races.

45    "1er mai 1899: La voiture electrique <<Jamais Content>> pulverise le record du monde de vitesse." Autoreduc.com. May 1, 2013. http://blog.autoreduc.com/1er-mai-1899-la-voiture-electrique-jamais-contente-pulverise-le-record-du-monde-de-vitesse/#.

46    Lions District 103.

47   Ray Stannard Baker, *The Boys' Book of Modern Inventions.* (McClure, Phillips & Co.: 1906), 130.

48   Ibid.

49   Sherman, "Original Speed Demon."

50   "The Long Island Automobile Club's Races." The Horseless Age 8, no. 34 (November 20, 1901): 735-739.

51   Vanderbilt Cup Races.

52   Michael W. Dominowski, "The crash of the Baker Electric Torpedo (Commentary)." Staten Island Advance. May 26, 2013. http://www.silive.com/opinion/columns/index.ssf/2013/05/the_crash_of_the_baker_electri.html.

53   Ibid.

54   Ibid.

55   "Automobile Club of New England's Track Races." The Horseless Age 8, no. 12 (June 19, 1901): 255-257.

56   Gary Smith. "Electric Baker Torpedo Racers." Dean's Garage, February 21, 2011, accessed May 21, 2015. http://deansgarage.com/2011/electric-baker-torpedo-racers/.

57   "An Electric Automobile Built Like a Drop of Oil." Popular Science, June 1916, 896.

58   "Full Steam Ahead—Leon Serpollet" The Old Motor, February 4, 2014, accessed January 10, 2016. http://theoldmotor.com/?p=113893

59   Ibid.

60   Smith, "Electric Baker Torpedo Racers."

61   Dominowski, "Crash of the Torpedo."

62   "Automobile Deals Death and Injury," New York Times, June 1, 1901.

63   Ibid.

64   "The Baker Electric Racing Automobile." Scientific American, June 14, 1902, 419.
65   NYT, "Automobile Deals Death."
66   "Another Death in Automobile Tragedy." New York Times, June 2, 1902.
67   NYT, "Automobile Deals Death."
68   Ibid.
69   SciAm, "The Baker Electric."
70   NYT, "Another Death."
71   Ibid.
72   Ibid.
73   SciAm, "The Baker Electric."
74   NYT, "Automobile Deals Death."
75   "The Cleveland Races." The Horseless Age 10, no. 12 (September 17, 1902): 317.
76   "The Cleveland Automobile Races." The Horseless Age 10, no. 13 (September 24, 1902): 335.
77   "The Races at Glenville Track, Cleveland." The Horseless Age 12, no. 11 (September 9, 1903): 287–290.
78   Panel discussion at the 2016 Faraday Future Formula E Long Beach race.
79   "Global Report on Urban Health," World Health Organization, 2016 accessed September 28, 2016. http://www.who.int/kobe_centre/measuring/urban-global-report/2016/en/.
80   Personal interviews, Long Beach, California, April 4, 2015.
81   Cherise Lapine, "10 Fastest Cars in the World," HowStuffWorks.com, accessed September 28, 2016. http://auto.howstuffworks.com/10-fastest-cars-in-the-world1.htm.
82   FIA World Land Speed Records, accessed Sep-

tember 28, 2016. http://www.fia.com/sports/fia-world-land-speed-records.

www.ingramcontent.com/pod-product-compliance
Lightning Source LLC
Chambersburg PA
CBHW021000090426
42736CB00010B/1400